Fresh & Fun

Halloween

BY TRACEY WEST

SCHOLASTIC
PROFESSIONAL BOOKS

NEW YORK • TORONTO • LONDON • AUCKLAND • SYDNEY

MEXICO CITY • NEW DELHI • HONG KONG

Edited by Joan Novelli
Front cover and interior design by Kathy Massaro
Cover and interior art by Paige Billin-Frye, except page 7 top by Dylan (grade 2),
bottom by Lauren (grade 2), and page 13 by Ellen Joy Sasaki

ISBN 0-439-05182-7

Contents

❖ Integrates Art

Introduction

Each year in October, many children are swept away by a rare kind of excitement. It seems that the first day of school is barely over before children eagerly begin anticipating Halloween. "What kind of costume will I wear?" "What will my friends dress as?" "Will I carve a pumpkin?" These and other Halloween thoughts seem to occupy children's minds for the entire month.

As a teacher, you know that any time children are excited about something, learning opportunities follow. That's the aim of this book: to provide you with a variety of fresh, fun activities inspired by the Halloween holiday that will tie into, and enrich, your K–2 curriculum.

In this book, you'll find fresh Halloween ideas from teachers around the country—simple to do, yet packed with learning potential. Some of the things you'll find in these pages include:

- ◎ a rhyming play to perform
- ◎ literature-based language arts activities
- ◎ story starters
- ◎ interactive bulletin boards
- ◎ hands-on math and science activities
- ◎ learning center suggestions
- ◎ graphic organizers
- ◎ reproducible student activity pages
- ◎ a great, big, colorful I Spy Spooky Nights poster, from the popular book by Jean Marzollo and Walter Wick
- ◎ and many more Halloween treats!

To make it easy for you to plan lessons that support your curriculum, the activities are organized by content areas. However, as you would expect in early elementary curriculum, most of the ideas naturally integrate a number of disciplines, giving you opportunities to engage all of your students' modes of expression. Children will draw, paint, play, create, think, research, share, and sing as they celebrate Halloween.

There are a number of ways you might choose to use the activities in this book. You might create a multidisciplinary unit of study by selecting an activity or two from each content area. You may choose instead to provide a Halloween focus in one particular discipline like math or language arts. Or, you may simply select a project here and there to add Halloween fun to your day.

Haunted Reading Corner

Make read-alone time more enticing with this simple center idea. Set up a table and a few chairs in one corner of the room. Make a spooky-looking sign that reads Haunted Reading Corner and hang it on the wall over the table. Stock the reading corner with read-alone books that have a Halloween theme.

Decorate the reading corner with Halloween items such as spider webs, plastic spiders, and hanging bats. (Check craft and party stores for decorations.) The center is also a great place to display students' Halloween artwork and projects as they are completed.

To keep track of students' reading activity at the center, you may wish to make multiple copies of a Halloween-themed reading response sheet, like the one shown here. Students can make Haunted Reading Corner folders by folding large construction paper in half. Other ways to use the Haunted Reading Corner follow.

- Gather children together for special, spooky read-alouds at the center. Turn off the lights to set the scene!

- Invite children to make and display posters featuring their favorite Halloween books.

- Make a chart or graph of the class's favorite books. (See page 11.)

- Use the corner as a place for children to complete individual activities, such as the Sticker Story Starters. (See page 6.)

- Make special Halloween stationery available to encourage children to write about the books they read. (See reproducible stationery, page 13.)

Spooky Stories

Name Ben   Date 10-31-98

I read a Halloween book called _____
Beneath the Ghost Moon

This story is about mice who are sleeping and crawly creatures that take their costumes.

I give this book a __5__ pumpkin rating.

Color in from one to five pumpkins
to show your rating.
Five pumpkins is the highest rating.

I Spy Spooky Nights: Teaching With the Poster

"I spy a broken bone and—BOO! A padlock, and 1892; A train, a chain, a busted seam, An eye of stone, and a silent SCREAM." *I Spy Spooky Nights*, by Jean Marzollo and Walter Wick (Scholastic, 1996), invites children into a haunted house and, in the I Spy tradition, challenges them to solve riddles on each page.

The poster (back of book) features a scene and riddle from this popular book. Display the poster, using sticky notes (trimmed to fit) to cover up the words *bat, cat, clock,* and *knock.* Write each of these words on a sticky note (trimmed to fit over the words) and let children take turns trying to complete the riddle. Then guide them in these I Spy activities.

Read the Rhyme.
What Can You Find?

I spy four pumpkins, a ruler, a bat,
Eight pinecones, a ladder, three acorns, a cat;

A scarecrow, a key, a clothespin, a clock,
Two bowling pins, and KNOCK, KNOCK, KNOCK!

SCHOLASTIC

◎ Solve the riddle by finding all the items mentioned. (Encourage children to keep their discoveries to themselves until everyone has had time to look.)

◎ Play a memory game. Let children take a good look at the poster. Then cover it up. How many different objects can they name? (Encourage children to take a close look. They'll be surprised at what the photographer uses to build each scene.)

◎ Clap out the beats in the riddle. Then work together to write a new I Spy rhyme. Draw a picture to go with the rhyme.

◎ Let children work in pairs to create their own Halloween I Spy pictures and riddles. Display them along a wall for some I Spy fun.

Make copies of the seasonal stationery on page 13 for students to use with any of the writing activities in this book. Another option for creating seasonal stationery is to use a program like Kid Pix Studio (Broderbund). Select clip art that suggests Halloween and "stamp" it to make a border on the page.

Sticker Story Starters

Fill a small box with a variety of Halloween stickers. (Look for inexpensive stickers at party supply, craft, and card stores.) Cut apart the stickers, leaving the backing intact. Let children choose stickers at random from the box and stick them on writing paper. Have children write short stories inspired by the pictures and/or words on the stickers.

Teacher Share

Collaborative Class Costume Book

My students enjoy telling me all about their costumes—in a book! I set aside a blank book and invite students to write descriptions of their costumes in it. They include as many details as they can, but don't tell me what their costumes are. I read their stories and write responses, guessing what the costumes are.

Diane Farnham
Orchard School
South Burlington, Vermont

Make My Monster

Students strengthen descriptive writing skills with this project, which you can adapt for use on the Internet. (See Computer Connection.)

◎ Ask students to each draw a picture of a monster. Encourage them to add details to their drawings.

◎ Have students write descriptions of their monsters (on new paper). Discuss the kinds of details they might want to include: What color is your monster? How big is it? How many arms and legs does it have? Does it have any unusual markings or parts?

◎ Pair up students and have them exchange descriptions only. Have students draw monsters based on their partners' written descriptions. When the drawings are complete, students compare them with their partners' originals to see how similar they are.

Book Break

The Hallo-Wiener
by Dav Pilkey (Scholastic, 1995)

Oscar is a dog who is "half a dog tall and one-and-a-half dogs long." Because he looks different, the other dogs make fun of him. This sweet and funny Halloween story is a great introduction for discussing issues such as friendship, and understanding that everyone is different. Use the book as a springboard for these activities, too.

◎ Make popsicle-stick puppets of the characters in the book and have students act out the play with their puppets as you read it aloud.

◎ In the beginning of the book, Oscar feels sad when the other dogs make fun of him. Have students write a letter to Oscar. What would they say?

◎ At the end of the book, Oscar saves the day when he reveals that the terrible pumpkin monster is really "two ornery cats." Is there another way the story might have ended? Have students write a new ending to the story, or write one together as a class.

Computer Connection

Make My Monster is an ideal project for use on the Internet. Team up your class with a class in another school. Have students send their descriptions via e-mail to their Internet partners. Students can compare drawings by scanning them and sending them as an e-mail attachment, by posting them at the class's or school's web site, or by sending them via regular mail.

Rhyming Bats Activity Board

The Halloween holiday is filled with rhyming words, and you can share them with students with this activity board.

◎ Make 18 photocopies of the upside-down bat pattern, below. (Enlarge it first.) On the bats, write the following rhyming words: *bat, cat, ghost, most, spider, cider, candy, dandy, treat, sweet, night, fright, beast, feast, scary, hairy, bone,* and *moan.*

◎ On a large piece of poster board draw a spooky tree with nine branches. Staple it to a bulletin board.

◎ Take nine bats (one from each pair), and staple them to the tree, one per branch, leaving room for rhyming partners next to each.

◎ Cut a small slit next to each hanging bat and slide the larger half of a paper clip into the slit.

◎ Staple an envelope to the board and store the remaining nine bats in it.

◎ Let students play at the board, trying to clip each bat next to its rhyming partner.

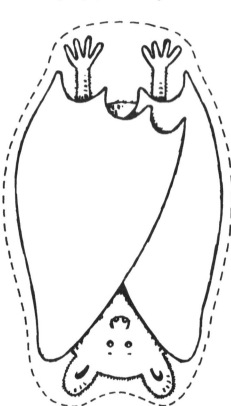

Spooky Story Bags

Judging from the wealth of children's books on Halloween, this is a subject that inspires storytellers. Let your students join the storytelling fun with Spooky Story Bags. Start by decorating several brown or white paper lunch bags. Place Halloween pictures (bats, ghosts, costumes, pumpkins, spiders, and so on) in a couple of bags. Label these bags "Spooky Story Pictures." Write Halloween words (*Boo!, night, creepy, trick, treat,* and so on) on orange slips of paper and place these in a couple of bags labeled "Spooky Story Words." Stock an extra couple of bags with special writing supplies, such as orange pens and pencils, pumpkin-shaped erasers, and copies of the Halloween stationery on page 13. Let children carry these mini writing centers back to their tables for writing fun, taking pictures and words at random from the bags and writing stories based on them.

Wonderful Word Webs

For fun vocabulary-building activities, try these spooky word webs.

A Web of Words Use the web-shaped reproducible on page 14 to create word webs. Start by making one copy of the reproducible. In the center of the web, write a Halloween word. Copy the page for students and let them add words around the web that relate to the center word. For example, if you're studying bats, write the word *bat* at the center. Words that children might fill in include *mammal, nocturnal, bugs, fruit, fly,* and *cave.*

Spider Word Webs Use the spider reproducible on page 15 to create word webs. Start by making one copy of the reproducible. In the spider's abdomen, write a Halloween-related word or other word of your choice. Make a class set of the page and have students write on the dotted lines as many words as they can think of that relate to the center word. For example, the word *Halloween* might generate such words as *costumes, candy, pumpkins, monsters, spiders, bats,* and *ghosts.*

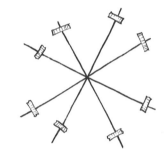

Variation For a special touch, make a giant spider word web to hang from a corner of the classroom.

◎ Cut five lengths of yarn, varying in size from $3\frac{1}{2}$ to 5 feet. (Modify this to fit your corner.)

◎ Tape four lengths of yarn to the wall so that the pieces intersect.

◎ Take the fifth length, tape one end to the wall, wrap it around the intersection of the first two strings, then attach the other end to the wall.

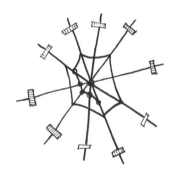

◎ Use additional yarn to create the spiral. Start by knotting the yarn close to the center. Move to the next radius, knot, and continue. Repeat until the web is complete.

◎ Write the word to be webbed on a card and tape it to the center of the web. Have children write related words on cards and tape them around the web.

Book Break

Halloween Cats

Jean Marzollo (Scholastic, 1992)

Invite young readers to chime in as you share this rhyming book about a group of mischievous trick-or-treating cats. Dim the lights before you read (and maybe put on a mask yourself). For an easy-to-perform play, let children make face masks to go with the cat characters and act out the story as you read it again.

Teacher Share

Comparing Bats and Birds

Children love *Stellaluna* by Janell Cannon (Harcourt Brace, 1993), the story of a baby fruit bat who is separated from her mother and is raised with a family of birds. Along the way, Stellaluna discovers that she and the birds are alike in many ways—and very different, too.

After reading *Stellaluna* with the class, make a Venn diagram comparing birds and fruit bats. Record the following information:

◎ things that are unique to birds (such as feathers, beaks, they like to eat bugs, they fly during the day, they sit right-side up). Write these in the left side of the diagram.

◎ things that are unique to fruit bats (such as no feathers, they like to eat fruit, they fly at night, they hang upside-down). Write these in the right side of the diagram.

◎ things that are common to birds and fruit bats (such as wings, they both fly). Write these in the center of the diagram.

Charlotte Sassman
Alice Carlson Applied Learning Center
Fort Worth, Texas

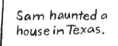

Sam haunted a house in Texas.

A man put up a reward for someone to stay in the house all night long.

Chef Dan came to the house.

Book Break

The Ghost of Sifty Sifty Sam

by Angela Shelf Madearis (Scholastic, 1997)

In this multicultural tale, a clever chef outwits a hungry ghost named Sifty Sifty Sam. After sharing the book, strengthen students' sequencing skills with an old-fashioned ghost-story session. Gather students in a circle. Begin retelling the story of Sifty Sifty Sam with a line such as, "Sam haunted a house in Texas." Write your line on chart paper. Invite the student to your left to tell what happened next, and write that down. Continue until the story has been retold in sequence. When you're done, you'll have completed a graphic organizer showing the story in sequence.

To extend the activity, copy each line on an index card and let students put them in order at a learning center.

Spooky Story Graphs

When you've read at least five Halloween books, create a graph to find out which was the class favorite. Write the names of five Halloween books on index cards and paste them to oaktag in a vertical column. Give each student an index card. Ask students to draw a scene from a favorite story on the card. Have students paste their cards on the graph in the appropriate row. Which book was their favorite? Which book was their least favorite? Would they like to read more books by their favorite author?

Halloween Night: A Rhyming Play

The reproducible play on pages 16–17 is a fun way to introduce Halloween concepts and vocabulary to students, as well as to explore rhyming words. Before performing the play, write key vocabulary on the chalkboard or distribute as a handout. Key vocabulary could include: *Halloween, night, fun, fright, trick, treat, bats, fly, high, sky, ghosts, boo, you, scare, monsters, scary, big, hairy, skeletons, bones, shrieks,* and *moans.* Encourage children to find the words that rhyme on the vocabulary list.

Give children time to practice in groups (trick-or-treaters, bats, ghosts, monsters, skeletons) before bringing them together for a rehearsal. Students can create some simple Halloween props, such as pumpkins cut out of cardboard and decorated, and then perform the play for an audience (such as another class). Use chart paper to create a big book based on the play. Write a different rhyming verse on each page of the book, and have groups of students illustrate the book.

Teacher Share

Characters in Costume

Favorite book characters are the inspiration for a festive day of dress-up in my classroom. My students write about their characters and their costumes. They share clues about their characters with classmates, who try to guess each other's identities. In the process, students learn a lot about the details that go into bringing story characters to life.

Jane Stilwell
Chapel Hill, North Carolina

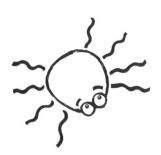

Ten Little Spiders

This poem and pocket chart activity will have children doing more than counting to ten (and subtracting). It's an invitation to play with rhyming words. Write each line of the poem on a sentence strip. Cut off the last word of each line. Arrange the sentence strips in order on a pocket chart. Place the individual words in the correct places and read the poem aloud with children. Then remove the last word of each line, mix them up, and invite children to take turns choosing words to complete the poem. After you've worked through the poem a couple of times so that each child has a chance to complete a line, place the pocket chart poem in a center and allow children to work with partners to put the poem together. You might cut up a few extra sentence strips for children who want to change the poem by adding their own rhyming words.

Ten Little Spiders

Ten little spiders went out one day,
Out on their spider's web to play.
Down flew a blackbird and gobbled up three,
Seven little spiders spun back to their tree.
Seven little spiders went out one day,
Out on their spider's web to play.
Along came a duster and whisked away four,
Three little spiders dropped back to the floor.
Three little spiders went out one day,
Out on their spider's web to play.
The wind came up and blew and blew,
One blew away and then there were two.
Two little spiders went out one day,
Out on their spider's web to play.
Two little spiders swinging in the sun,
Swung off their web and then there were none.

Valerie SchifferDanoff
Bedford Village Elementary
Bedford, New York

Adapted from *The Scholastic Integrated Language Arts Resource Book* by Valerie SchifferDanoff (Scholastic Professional Books, 1995)

Activity Page

Name _____ Date _____

Name _____ Date _____

A Web of Words

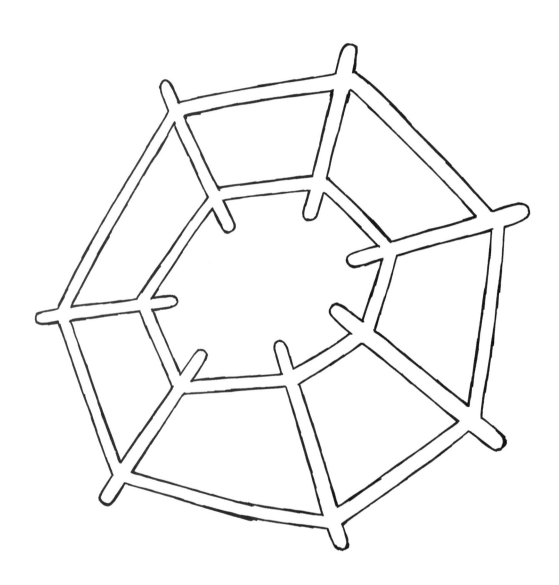

Name _____   Date _____

Spider Word Web

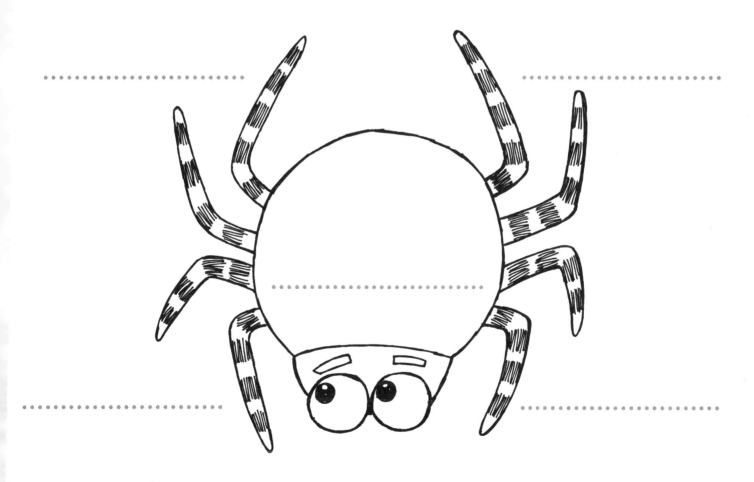

Halloween Night

A Rhyming Play

Characters
(to be played by small groups of students):

Trick-or-treaters ★ Bats ★ Ghosts ★ Monsters ★ Skeletons

Setting: A neighborhood. There is a "house" or door on stage left which the trick-or-treaters will repeatedly visit.

Trick-or-treaters (facing audience):	Halloween night. Halloween night. Full of fun. Full of fright.

The trick-or-treaters walk to the door of the house and ring the bell.

Trick-or-treaters:	Trick or treat! It's Halloween night. Are you fun? Or are you a fright?
Bats (flapping their wings):	We are bats. We can fly. We fly high In the Halloween sky.

Trick-or-treaters (running away): Eeeeeeek!

The bats fly off stage. The trick-or-treaters walk back to the door of the house and ring the bell.

Trick-or-treaters:	Trick or treat! It's Halloween night. Are you fun? Or are you a fright?
Ghosts:	We are ghosts. We say, "Boo!" On Halloween night We will scare you!

Trick-or-treaters (running away): Eeeeeeek!

Fresh & Fun Halloween Scholastic Professional Books

The ghosts float off stage. The trick-or-treaters walk back to the door of the house and ring the bell.

Trick-or-treaters:

Trick or treat!
It's Halloween night.
Are you fun?
Or are you a fright?

**Monsters
(raising their arms in the air):**

We are monsters.
We are scary.
We are big
And very hairy!

Trick-or-treaters (running away): Eeeeeeek!

The monsters stomp off stage. The trick-or-treaters walk back to the door of the house and ring the bell.

Trick-or-treaters:

Trick or treat!
It's Halloween night.
Are you fun?
Or are you a fright?

Skeletons:

We are skeletons
Made of bones.
Hear our shrieks.
Hear our moans.

Trick-or-treaters (running away): Eeeeeeek!

The skeletons rattle off stage. The trick-or-treaters face the audience.

Trick-or-treaters:

Halloween night.
Halloween night.
Full of fun.
Full of fright.

The night is over.
Halloween is done.
We were scared,
But we had fun!

 The End

Teacher Share

Math-o-Ween

On the Friday before Halloween, our school holds a Math-o-Ween extravaganza. Each class is responsible for a booth in the hallway (usually around a table or two). At the booth, which is run by children, visitors can play a math game. Many classes invent new games for the event.

Here's one example of a Math-o-Ween game: "Flip the Cards" is played like the traditional "War" card game. Make 30 cards, each with a different math addition fact. Divide the cards evenly among 2–3 players. Each child turns over two cards, adds them together, and the child with the largest sum keeps the cards in that round. The child with the most cards at the end of the game wins.

We also have a costume contest on Math-o-Ween. The twist? All costumes must have a math theme. As you can probably guess, Count Dracula is a favorite!

Charlotte Sassman
Alice Carlson Applied Learning Center
Fort Worth, Texas

Book Break

Scary, Scary Halloween
by Eve Bunting (Clarion, 1986)

"I peer outside, there's something there
That makes me shiver, spikes my hair.
It must be Halloween…"

In this classic rhyming story, unseen observers hide in the shadows and watch the scary, spooky creatures that come out on Halloween night. Throughout the book, grinning jack-o-lanterns shine through the darkness, each with a different expression. After reading, challenge students to create their own scary pumpkin masks using geometric shapes. Provide paper plates for the masks. Help children cut out holes for their eyes and mouth, then let them use construction paper cut into geometric shapes to decorate their masks. Punch holes on either side of each mask and string with yarn. Follow up by using the quantity graph template on page 25 to graph the shapes students used to make their masks.

Sweet Sorting

For many children, candy is the best thing about Halloween. Why not use these sweet treats to enrich a math lesson? If you are going to serve candy at your Halloween party, use the candy for a sorting exercise before kids dig in.

Have students work in small groups. Give each group a bowl or dish filled with a variety of small candy—about 10 or 20 pieces—and several empty paper cups. Encourage children to find as many ways to sort the candy as they can. To extend the activity, have students keep a record of sorting results each time (3 round, 2 square, 4 rectangles, etc.) and use this information to make simple graphs.

You may want to follow this candy-sorting activity with a review of the things kids need to do to maintain good dental health!

TIP

If you would prefer to do this activity without the actual candy, you can have children cut out pictures from grocery store flyers and use those to sort.

Book Break

Two Little Witches: A Halloween Counting Story

by Harriet Ziefert (Candlewick Press, 1996)

"If four trick-or-treaters meet one striped cat, that makes…[page is turned] five trick-or-treaters in the dark on Halloween night." This trick-or-treat tale is a perfect opportunity to practice simple addition and subtraction. In this story, one trick-or-treater is joined one-by-one by others. The book is written so that children can add and subtract on their own.

You may wish to read the book aloud, writing each math equation on the board as you go. Before you turn each page, challenge children to solve the problem. Then use the book to create a fun folder activity.

◎ Draw pictures of the ten trick-or-treaters on ten index cards (one per card) and put them in a pocket on the right side of a folder. On the pocket, write "Use the trick-or-treaters to help you find the answers."

◎ Write addition and subtraction equations on additional index cards and place them in a pocket on the left side of the folder. On the pocket, write "Pick a card."

◎ Have students choose cards from the left pocket and use the cards in the right pocket as manipulatives to help them find the answers. Instruct students to write their equations and answers on a separate sheet of paper.

Monster Math Bulletin Board

The friendly Frankenstein monster template on page 24 makes a great interactive bulletin board and is a fun way to review fact families. Make multiple photocopies of the monster and cut out the body, arms, and legs. On each body, write a different number. Then write a math fact that corresponds to that number on each arm and each leg. (Laminate these parts for durability, if possible.) For example:

On body:	7	On left leg:	3 + 4
On left arm:	5 + 2	On right leg:	6 + 1
On right arm:	7 + 0		

When you are done marking up the monsters, staple the monster bodies onto the bulletin board, leaving enough room around each one to attach arms and legs. Place the arms and legs in a folder and staple it to the bulletin board. Invite children to become "mad scientists" and complete the monsters by attaching the correct arms and legs. Several ways to attach body parts include:

◎ Punch holes in the body and arms and legs and have children use paper fasteners to connect them.

◎ Provide thumbtacks to attach parts.

◎ Attach Velcro squares to the backs of the arms and legs and to the corresponding spots on the monster bodies.

This activity can be easily adapted for use with other kinds of math facts, and could also be used as a language arts activity. (For example, you can write individual words on the body and synonyms on the arms and legs. Students match arms and legs to monster bodies by figuring out which words go together.) If you don't have the space for an interactive bulletin board, store the monster parts in folders and make them available at a learning center.

Little Count Dracula

How do you teach counting during Halloween? With Count Dracula, of course! Each day in October, assign one student the title of Little Count Dracula. For that day, that student will be called on to count different things in the classroom: the number of students in line, the number of books on a shelf, the number of legs on a desk, and so on. If you wish, decorate a square of cloth with numbers, plus signs, and minus signs, and let Little Count Dracula wear this math cape for the day.

Teacher Share

Spooky Ice Cream Surprises

With a few toppings and a scoop of ice cream, students can make spooky sundaes for a Halloween treat. Start by freezing individual scoops of ice cream on waxed paper. (This will give children more time to create their sundaes before the ice cream starts to melt.) While the ice cream scoops freeze, set up sundae stations for small groups of children. Place small dishes filled with toppings such as candy corn, sugar cones, sprinkles, strips of licorice, gumdrops, and other goodies at each station. Have some whipped cream on hand, too. Give each child a scoop of ice cream in a paper bowl, and a spoon. Then let everyone go to work, creating witches (an upside-down cone makes a great hat), pumpkins, goblins...whatever Halloween brings to mind. Be sure to give children a few minutes to admire one another's creations before they dig in! Follow up by inviting children to write recipes for making their sundaes. Encourage them to use numbers to tell how many and how much.

Lynn Vesely
Wildwood School
Amherst, Massachusetts

Book Break

The 13 Nights of Halloween
by Rebecca Dickinson (Scholastic, 1996)

This spooky twist on the traditional Christmas song is a natural introduction to a graphing activity. On a large piece of posterboard, create a vertical column of the numbers 1–13 (bottom to top). Across (left to right), create a row of the 13 different gifts mentioned in the book (in order): owl, toads, jack-o-lanterns, witches, pounds of worms, spiders, lizards, werewolves, bats, skeletons, black cats, vampires, and ghosts. Draw lines to create a 13-by-13 grid.

Let students help you put an "X" in each square to indicate the number of gifts given in each category. When you are done, ask students to estimate how many gifts in all one goblin gave to the other. Add the numbers together to find the answer.

Teacher Share

Patterns in a Pot

A Halloween cauldron filled with creepy critters is the centerpiece of this math activity, which works well at a learning center or work table. Find a large pot (such as a plastic cauldron you might find at a party or craft store). Fill the pot with an assortment of small plastic Halloween toys, such as plastic spiders, ghosts, pumpkins, eyeballs, and snakes. You'll also need a dipper, such as a soup ladle, for students to scoop up the critters.

Place the pot of critters on a table. Next to the pot, provide pattern "recipes" written on index cards. A sample recipe follows.

Spider Stew

Take two scoops of critters. Then make this pattern:

2 spiders, 2 ghosts, 1 snake

Repeat the pattern three times, adding one more scoop if necessary.

Encourage students to invent new patterns, then write their own recipes on index cards and challenge other students to follow them. Students can also use the pot of critters to sort the contents in different ways, or create picture or object graphs that show how many different kinds of critters are in the pot. For a language arts connection, have students scoop a small number of critters from the pot and write a short story about the creatures.

Valerie SchifferDanoff
Bedford Village Elementary
Bedford, New York

Adapted from *The Scholastic Integrated Language Arts Resource Book* by Valerie SchifferDanoff (Scholastic Professional Books, 1995)

Pumpkin Patch Bulletin Board

This activity is a great way to begin the month of October. Before October 1, make 31 photocopies of the pumpkin pattern below. (Or use the template as a pattern and have children trace it and cut out the pumpkins.) Write a math fact that represents each day of the month on each of the pumpkins, or assign each student in the class a different day of the month to come up with the fact for that day. (For example, you can write the math fact 12 − 11 for October 1, 9 − 7 for October 2, 0 + 3 for October 3, and so on. Write the answer for each equation on the back of the pumpkin. Staple the pumpkins to the bulletin board in random order. Use green construction paper vines and leaves to turn the board into a pumpkin patch, if you wish.

Each day in October, challenge students to identify the pumpkin that correctly represents that day. (On Mondays, you might wish to include the weekend days, too.) Ask students to write their choices on slips of paper and place them in a box or plastic pumpkin that you pass around. Invite the student who wrote the math fact for that day to turn over the correct pumpkin. Review the box of guesses to see who guessed correctly.

Here are some other ways to use the pumpkin patch:

◎ Each day, challenge students to come up with additional facts that equal that day's date.

◎ At the end of the month, have students harvest the pumpkins and try to arrange them in sequence from 1–31.

◎ Invite students to count pumpkins by twos or fives. How many groups of each are there? How many extra pumpkins are there?

Adapted from *Interactive Bulletin Boards: Math* by Judy Meagher and Joan Novelli (Scholastic Professional Books, 1998)

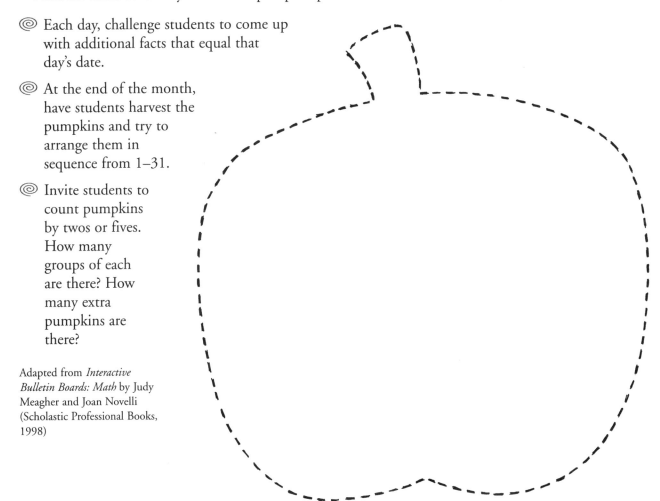

Monster Math

Name _____ Date _____

Scary, Scary Halloween

How many of each shape did you use? Draw the shape as many times as you used it.

● Circles	■ Squares
▬ Rectangles	▲ Triangles

Teacher Share

Three Generations of Halloween

Most adults have favorite memories of Halloweens past. Students can learn about life in the past by interviewing adults of two different generations—such as a mother and a grandmother—about the Halloweens of their childhoods. Encourage students to ask such questions as:

◎ What was your favorite costume?

◎ What special things did you do to celebrate Halloween?

◎ What was the most exciting thing to happen to you on Halloween?

Students can use the reproducible on page 32 to draw pictures of themselves in costume, as well as the adults (as children) whom they interviewed. You may also wish to have students share their interviews aloud with the class, and then recreate a favorite activity of Halloween past, such as bobbing for apples (use a separate container for each child).

Marjorie Hauck
Babylon Elementary School
Babylon, New York

Safety First

At Halloween time, discussing safety issues with children is not only appropriate, it's often necessary. If possible, invite a member of your local police department to come talk to your class about Halloween safety. Follow up by having children work together to make Halloween safety posters. Tips might include:

◎ Never trick-or-treat alone. Always go with an adult.

◎ Bring a flashlight.

◎ Wear reflective strips on clothing.

◎ Make sure you can see clearly in your costume. Instead of a mask, wear face paint.

◎ Don't enter anyone's house while trick-or-treating, even if you're invited in.

◎ Have an adult check your candy before you eat it.

Display posters in a hallway to share your safety lesson with the school.

Book Break

Day of the Dead
by Tony Johnston (Harcourt Brace, 1997)

On November 1, most American children are putting away their costumes and polishing off their candy. In Mexico, a special celebration is beginning. This book lovingly describes the step-by-step preparations for the Mexican holiday known as the Day of the Dead. On this holiday, Mexican families honor their dead ancestors by preparing special foods and visiting the graves of loved ones. Children eat *calaveras de azucar*—sugar skulls.

After sharing the story, have children locate Mexico on a map. Challenge students to answer the following questions: *In what direction would we have to go to reach Mexico from our school? Through which states would we travel to get to Mexico? Which U.S. states border Mexico?*

If any of your students are from Mexico or have families from Mexico, encourage them to share what they know about the country. Have they ever celebrated the Day of the Dead? What other kinds of celebrations do they have in Mexico?

Teacher Share

Alike or Different?

Pumpkins are easy to distinguish from other fruits: They're much bigger than most and have a distinctive stem. In fact, they don't seem to have much in common at all with other fruit. I have my students compare pumpkins with oranges to decide for themselves. I start by putting a pumpkin in one bag and an orange in another. I staple the bags closed and pass them around, asking students to use their senses to gather clues about what's inside. After everyone makes a guess, we open the bags. I then challenge students to find five ways the pumpkins and oranges are alike. After they've had plenty of time to compare the pumpkin and orange on the outside, I cut open the fruit and students continue with their comparisons. Once each student has had time to record five ways the fruits are alike, we share findings for a class chart. Together, students discover that pumpkins have many things in common with other fruit.

Lynne Kepler
Clarion Limestone Elementary School
Strattanville, Pennsylvania

It's Pumpkin Time!
by Zoe Hall (Scholastic, 1994)

This friendly book follows the excitement of a brother and sister as they plant pumpkin seeds, care for the growing plants, pick the pumpkins, and then carve them into jack-o-lanterns. It's a wonderful introduction to the subject of pumpkins and seeds. After reading the book with the class, you may wish to try one of these science activities.

Using pumpkin seeds from a packet, have each student plant a pumpkin seed in a paper cup full of potting soil. You could choose to experiment with the seeds to determine the best conditions for getting the seeds to sprout. Put some seeds on a sunny windowsill, and others in a dark closet; water some seeds once a day, and others once a week. Or, simply let children sprout their seeds and watch the plants grow. Have children staple blank paper together to make science journals and use words and/or pictures to record daily observations.

Teacher Share

Spooky Shadow Science

Set up this spooky shadow center to help children discover the science of shadows.

◎ Cut the top flaps off a large cardboard box. Have children paint the outside black and decorate with Halloween motifs.

◎ Let children decorate the inside of the box. They might, for example, pull apart cotton balls and glue the wispy material to corners, or cut yarn into pieces to make spider webs. Have children cut out Halloween shapes, such as ghosts and cats, and glue them to craft sticks to make shadow puppets.

◎ Darken the room. Shine a flashlight on the interior of the box, while children move their puppets in front of the light source. Discuss what happens to the shadows as children move them closer to and farther from the light source.

Janet Fuller
The Children's School
South Burlington, Vermont

Teacher Share

Sinking Surprises

Use pumpkins to explore things that float and things that sink. Fill a garbage can with water (outdoors works best), and start with one pumpkin. Ask students to make guesses about whether or not the pumpkin will float. Kids might be surprised to find that a heavy pumpkin doesn't sink to the bottom, due to its density. After you try the pumpkin, ask students to brainstorm a list of other fruits they would like to test. (Encourage, but don't limit their choices to other fall produce, such as squash, cranberries, and oranges.) In my classroom, students were amazed that a grape was the only fruit to sink, while a 20-pound pumpkin actually floated.

Wendy Weiner
53rd Street School
Milwaukee, Wisconsin

Pumpkin History

Young children might associate pumpkins with one thing only—jack-o-lanterns—but people have been eating pumpkins for hundreds of years. Early Americans cut off the tops of pumpkins, scooped out the seeds, and filled them with a mixture of milk, spices, and sugar. They popped the tops back on and baked their pumpkins over a fire for a delicious treat. (Try this with your students if you have access to an oven. Children will have fun guessing what will happen to the ingredients as they bake.)

Invite students to find out other ways people have used pumpkins over the years. Cut out pumpkin-shaped pages and invite each child to contribute a page to a collaborative book about pumpkin history.

Pumpkin Facts

After completing all these pumpkin activities, your students will be pumpkin experts! They can show off their knowledge with a pumpkin facts bulletin board.

Students can trace the pumpkin pattern on page 23 on a sheet of orange construction paper that is folded in half. Instruct students not to cut the stem, so that the pumpkin face can be lifted up. Students can decorate the top flap with a jack-o-lantern face. Inside the pumpkin, they can write a pumpkin fact. Tack the finished pumpkins to a bulletin board or wall outside the classroom to share with others.

Teacher Share

Pumpkin Muffins

These easy muffins give me a chance to explore the science of change with my students. As we follow the directions, I ask students to make observations both before and after mixing ingredients together. At each step, I ask: *How have the ingredients changed?* While the muffins bake, students share their own "recipes" for making muffins.

Ingredients

2 eggs
$1\frac{1}{2}$ cups milk
4 tablespoons oil
1 cup cooked (or canned) pumpkin

1 cup sugar
$1\frac{1}{4}$ teaspoons pumpkin pie spice
4 cups biscuit mix

Directions
Mix together the eggs, milk, and oil. Add the pumpkin, sugar, and pie spice. Stir, then add the biscuit mix and combine. Spoon into greased muffin tins. Bake at 350° F. for about 25 minutes. Makes 2 dozen muffins. (If you use mini-muffin tins, baking time will decrease.)

Lynne Kepler
Clarion Limestone Elementary School
Strattanville, Pennsylvania

TIP

If your students are interested in learning more about spiders and bats, try these teacher resources.

Spiders by Rhonda Lucas Donald and Kathleen W. Kranking (Scholastic Professional Books, 1999) has hands-on reproducibles, cross-curricular activities, games, art projects, a colorful poster, and other material for teaching about arachnids.

Bats by Robin Bernard (Scholastic Professional Books, 1998) is a complete cross-curricular theme unit that includes background information, reproducible activity pages, and a big bat poster.

Book Break

Miss Spider's ABC

by David Kirk (Scholastic, 1998)

Many Halloween stories emphasize a fear of "creepy crawly" things such as spiders. This is a good time of year to show students that when we know the truth about things, they aren't so scary anymore. *Miss Spider's ABC* is a great introduction to all kinds of insects, and can lead into a variety of activities.

◎ Miss Spider is an arachnid, and many of the creatures in this book are insects. Create a Venn diagram that shows ways arachnids and insects are alike and different. (Arachnids have eight legs, insects have six legs; insects and arachnids are both invertebrates; arachnids have a body divided into two parts, insects have a body divided into three parts; etc.)

○ Make a chart with two columns: INSECTS WE HAVE SEEN and INSECTS WE HAVE NOT SEEN. Discuss the insects in the book and fill in the chart based on the experiences of students in your class.

○ Approach the story one letter at a time. Are there other insects that could have been included, such as "beetle" instead of "bumblebee"? Brainstorm a list of additional insects and write and illustrate your own insect alphabet book.

Bat Facts

Like spiders, bats are another creature that often inspire fear, especially at Halloween. However, bats are actually very beneficial creatures that are rarely harmful to humans. Discuss bat facts and myths with your students. (You can use the information provided here or conduct research with students.) Then turn the lesson into a folder activity. Write each fact and myth on an index card. On the back of the fact cards, write "Fact." On the backs of the myth cards, write "Myth." Shuffle the cards to mix up facts with myths. Set up a pocket folder for sorting the cards, one side labeled "Bat Facts," the other "Bat Myths." Challenge students to sort the cards into their correct pockets. They can check their work when they're done by looking at the backs of the cards. (During the lesson, you may wish to remind students that although only a very small percentage of bats carry rabies, you should never touch a bat if you see one.)

Trick-or-Treat for UNICEF

Kids across the country trick-or-treat for UNICEF (United Nations Children's Fund), founded in 1946 to help children in developing countries. To educate your students about the important work of UNICEF, and to show them how they can make a difference, too, try these activities.

○ Locate developing countries, such as Namibia, Zambia, Mozambique, Liberia, El Salvador, and Vietnam on a map. Help children learn what life is like for many children in these countries by asking: *What do you do when you want a drink of water? What would you do if you had to go to a river every day for water? How would you know if the water was safe to drink?* (Guide children to understand that clean water is scarce in these countries, and that millions of children die each year from drinking unclean water.)

○ Explain that the money raised for UNICEF helps purify drinking water in developing countries. Ask: *What are some ways we can raise money to help UNICEF?* Trick-or-Treating for UNICEF is one way. Others ideas include holding an Estimation Raffle (fill a jar with candy corn and sell chances to guess the number of pieces of candy in the jar) and organizing a student/teacher soccer or baseball game (charge admission and ask local businesses to donate refreshments).

For more information about UNICEF, call (800)FOR-KIDS.

Bat Facts

○ One little brown bat can eat 1,200 mosquitoes and other insects in one hour.

○ Big brown bats help farmers by eating insects that harm crops.

○ Bats in the rain forest spread pollen from flower to flower, which helps new flowers grow.

○ Bats can see, but they also rely on a sense called *sonar* to find their way at night.

○ Most bats eat insects, and many bats eat fruit.

○ Bats like to live with other bats, not near people.

Bat Myths

○ All bats carry disease that they give to humans and animals.

○ Bats are blind.

○ All bats are vampires and drink human blood.

○ Bats often become tangled in human hair.

○ Bats like to live near people.

Three Generations of Halloween

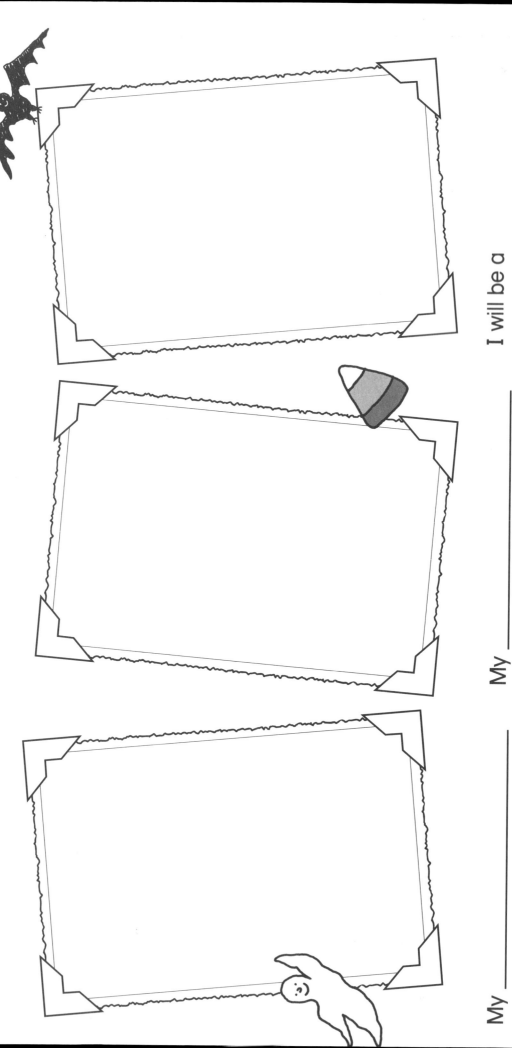

My _____   My _____   I will be a

was a _____.   was a _____.   _____.